SAUTÉED CABBAGE

An economical vegetable. It has a very faint hint of sauerkraut flavor.

Chopped or sliced onion	¾ cup	175 mL
Water		
Grated cabbage, packed	4 cups	900 mL
Vegetable cooking oil	1 tbsp.	15 mL
Vinegar	1 tbsp.	15 mL

Combine onion and water in frying pan. Cover. Add more water if needed. Simmer until soft.

Add cabbage. Stir. Add more water if needed. Simmer until cabbage is tender crisp.

Add cooking oil and vinegar. Stir-fry about 20 to 25 minutes until liquid and water has boiled away. Makes 2 cups (450 mL).

½ cup 125 mL contains:	
Energy	61 Calories (254 kJ)
Cholesterol	
Sodium	0 mg
Fat	14 mg
	4 g

Taste the Tradition

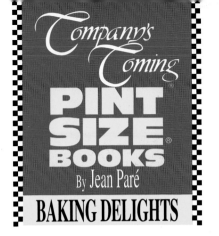

Company's Coming
PINT SIZE BOOKS®
By Jean Paré
BAKING DELIGHTS

Third Printing August 1995

ISBN 1-895455-38-3

Published and Distributed by
Company's Coming Publishing Limited
Box 8037, Station "F"
Edmonton, Alberta, Canada
T6H 4N9

**Published Simultaneously in
Canada and the United States of America**

Front and Back Cover Photo

1. Gumdrop Loaf page 46
2. Orange Chocolate Cake page 22
3. Hawaiian Cake page 19
4. Tassies page 56
5. Snow Drops page 26
6. Cherry Bran Loaf page 45
7. Date Pie page 61
8. Chocolate Amaretto Cheesecake page 39
9. Cranberry Orange Muffins page 50
10. Fruitcake Cookies page 29
11. Sweet Pastry Pie page 57
12. Pompadour Pudding page 34
13. Christmas Stollen page 12

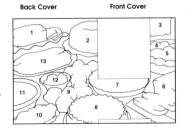

Printed In Canada

Tablecloth Courtesy Of: Ikea
Trays Courtesy Of: Ali Katu
Blue Glassware Courtesy Of: Eaton's
Blue China Courtesy Of: Enchanted Kitchen
Red Platter Courtesy Of: Le Gnome

The Jean Paré Story

Jean Paré grew up understanding that the combination of family, friends and home cooking is the essence of a good life. When she left home she took with her many acquired family recipes, her love of cooking and her intriguing desire to read recipe books like novels! While raising a family of four, Jean was always busy in her kitchen preparing delicious, tasty treats and savory meals for family and friends of all ages. Her reputation flourished as the mom who would happily feed the neighborhood.

In 1963, when her children had all reached school age, Jean volunteered to cater to the 50th anniversary of the Vermilion School of Agriculture, now Lakeland College, in the town of Vermilion, Alberta, Canada. Working out of her home, Jean prepared a dinner for over 1000 people which launched a flourishing catering operation that continued for over eighteen years. During that time she was provided with countless opportunities to test new ideas with immediate feedback – resulting in empty plates and contented customers! Whether preparing cocktail sandwiches for a house party or serving a hot meal for 1500 people, Jean Paré earned a reputation for good food, courteous service and reasonable prices.

"Why don't you write a cookbook?" Time and again, as requests for her recipes mounted, Jean was asked that question. Jean's response was to team up with her son Grant Lovig in the fall of 1980 to form Company's Coming Publishing Limited. April 14, 1981, marked the debut of "150 DELICIOUS SQUARES", the first Company's Coming cookbook in what soon would become Canada's most popular cookbook series. Popularity of the series spread to the United States and overseas markets. French and Spanish language versions were first published in 1990.

Pint Size Books followed in 1993, offering a smaller less expensive format focussing on more specialized topics. The recipes continued in the familiar and trusted Company's Coming style.

Jean Paré's approach to cooking has always called for quick and easy recipes using everyday ingredients. Her wonderful collection of time-honored recipes, many of which are family heirlooms, is a welcome addition to any kitchen. That's why we say: "taste the tradition".

Table Of Contents

Foreword

"Oohs" and "aahs" are sure to be heard when the aroma of fresh baking fills your home. Baking Delights will inspire both experienced and novice cooks with a heavenly assortment of baking recipes.

Homemade biscuits, muffins, and buns have special appeal for mid-morning coffee, or as a busy day snack. Peanut Butter Biscuits, Chocolate Bran Muffins, or King Scones are made with remarkable ease, giving tantalizing results. There are simple, traditional "scratch" recipes as well as recipes using convenient mixes for scrumptious desserts. Orange Chocolate Cake is sinfully rich-tasting. With a luscious tunnel of chocolate orange filling, it really tastes as wonderful as it looks. The Hawaiian Cake is made so easily – a three-tiered delicacy with an impressive look. These fabulous cakes will bring a smile to anyone celebrating a birthday. You may want to try something different and put candles on the Cappuccino Cheesecake!

Entertaining a crowd or hosting a tea calls for breads, loaves, sweets and squares. The delectable selection of cookies, in all shapes, sizes and flavors, rounds off a tray of goodies or fills any family's cookie jar.

All recipes in Baking Delights freeze well, unless noted otherwise. Why not bake up a storm and freeze a selection of treats to have on hand? With the greatest of ease you will satisfy every sweet occasion – perfect planning for unexpected guests, or for a quick and easy self-indulgence.

Whatever your pleasure, each of the recipes is sweet and satisfying. From splendidly rich desserts to melt-in-your-mouth morsels, there is a temptation for everyone in Baking Delights.

Jean Paré

King Scone

A cream cheese and raisin filling is the special treat for this SKAHN. Decadent.

250 g	8 oz.	Cream cheese, softened	Beat cheese and sugar together well. Stir in raisins and lemon rind. Set aside.
125 mL	½ cup	Granulated sugar	
125 mL	½ cup	Raisins or currants	
5 mL	1 tsp.	Grated lemon rind	
750 mL	3 cups	All-purpose flour	Place flour, baking powder and salt in bowl. Cut in butter until fine and crumbly. Make a well.
20 mL	4 tsp.	Baking powder	
5 mL	1 tsp.	Salt	
125 mL	½ cup	Cold butter or hard margarine	
1	1	Large egg	Beat egg in small bowl. Add milk. Stir. Pour into well. Stir to form soft dough. Do not knead. Divide dough in four. Pat each piece into a circle, about 6 inches (15 cm) in diameter. Place 2 circles on greased baking sheet. Spread cheese mixture over top. Cover with other 2 circles.
250 mL	1 cup	Milk	
		Granulated sugar, sprinkle	Sprinkle lightly with granulated sugar. Bake in 425°F (220°C) oven for 15 to 20 minutes until browned. Each scone cuts into 8 to 10 wedges.

Pictured on page 11.

Peanut Butter Biscuits

Now all you need is the jelly for these tasty little biscuits.

500 mL	2 cups	All-purpose flour
15 mL	1 tbsp.	Baking powder
2 mL	½ tsp.	Salt
60 mL	¼ cup	Butter or hard margarine
60 mL	¼ cup	Smooth peanut butter
250 mL	1 cup	Milk

Combine first 3 ingredients in bowl. Stir. Cut in butter and peanut butter until crumbly. Make a well in center.

Pour milk into well. Stir to make soft ball. Knead 8 to 10 times on lightly floured surface. If dough is sticky, work a bit of flour into it as you knead. Pat or roll ¾ inch (2 cm) thick. Cut into 2 inch (5 cm) rounds. Place on ungreased baking sheet. Bake in 450°F (230°C) oven for 10 to 12 minutes. Makes 16 biscuits.

Pictured below.

1. Peanut Butt
   Biscuits pag
2. Potato Bun
   page 9

Basket Courtesy Of:
Stokes

Potato Buns

Soft, tender and easy. You will need to save water in which you have cooked potatoes.

125 mL	½ cup	Butter or hard margarine
125 mL	½ cup	Granulated sugar
2 mL	½ tsp.	Salt
175 mL	¾ cup	Hot potato water (drained from cooked potatoes)

Stir first 4 ingredients in large bowl until butter melts. Cool.

2	2	Large eggs, beaten
900 mL	4 cups	All-purpose flour
1 x 8 g	1 x ¼ oz.	Instant yeast granules (1 tbsp., 15 mL)

Add beaten eggs. Stir. Add flour and yeast. Mix. Knead on lightly floured surface until shiny and elastic feeling. Place in greased bowl, turning so both sides are greased. Cover with tea towel. Let rise about 2 hours until double in bulk. Punch down. Shape into buns. Arrange on greased pan. Let rise to double size. Bake in 375°F (190°C) oven for about 15 minutes until browned. Makes 20 buns.

Pictured on page 8.

Confetti Biscuits

Fruity and very good. A special treat for tea or lunch.

625 mL	2½ cups	All-purpose flour
7 mL	1½ tsp.	Cream of tartar
4 mL	¾ tsp.	Baking soda
4 mL	¾ tsp.	Salt
60 mL	¼ cup	Butter or hard margarine
125 mL	½ cup	Cut mixed glazed fruit, chopped fine
250 mL	1 cup	Milk

Combine flour, cream of tartar, baking soda and salt in bowl. Stir well. Cut in butter until mixture is mealy.

Add fruit and milk. Stir to form soft ball. Knead about 6 times on lightly floured surface. Roll or pat ¾ inch (2 cm) thick. Cut into 2 inch (5 cm) circles. Arrange on greased baking sheet. Bake in 450°F (230°C) oven for 10 to 12 minutes until risen and browned. Yields 16 biscuits.

Pictured on page 11.

1. Confetti Biscuits page 10
2. Fruity Oatmeal Muffins page 54
3. Good Morning Muffins page 51
4. Blueberry Lemon Muffins page 55
5. King Scone page 7
6. Brazil Loaf page 42

Jam Jar Courtesy Of:
Dansk Gifts

China Courtesy Of:
The Royal Doulton Store

Wire Baskets Courtesy OF:
Stokes

Napkin Courtesy Of:
Enchanted Kitchen

Christmas Stollen

Make the quick bread method rather than using yeast. Especially good warm.

600 mL	2½ cups	All-purpose flour	Put first 6 ingredients into
125 mL	½ cup	Ground almonds	large bowl. Add butter. Cut
60 mL	¼ cup	Granulated sugar	in until crumbly.
15 mL	1 tbsp.	Baking powder	
2 mL	½ tsp.	Salt	
1 mL	¼ tsp.	Nutmeg	
175 mL	¾ cup	Butter or margarine, cold	
250 mL	1 cup	Creamed cottage cheese	Put cottage cheese, egg
1	1	Large egg	and 3 flavorings into
5 mL	1 tsp.	Almond flavoring	blender. Purée. Pour into
5 mL	1 tsp.	Rum flavoring	flour mixture.
5 mL	1 tsp.	Vanilla	

Continued on next page.

❶

❷

125 mL	½ cup	Currants
60 mL	¼ cup	Candied cut lemon peel
60 mL	¼ cup	Candied cherries, quartered

❶ Add currants, peel and cherries. Stir into dry mixture to form a ball. Knead 8 times on lightly floured surface. ❷ Roll into oval shape 10 inches (25 cm) long and 8 inches (20 cm) wide. About ¾ inch (2 cm) off center lengthwise, use dull edge of knife to cut about ¼ inch (6 mm) deep. This makes it easier to bend. ❸ Fold narrower side over. It will look like a big long parkerhouse roll. Place on ungreased baking sheet. Bake in 350°F (175°C) oven for about 45 to 50 minutes or until an inserted wooden pick comes out clean.

| 5 mL | 1 tsp. | Butter or hard margarine, melted |
| | | Icing (confectioner's) sugar, sprinkle |

❹ Brush with melted butter. Sift icing sugar over top. This is better if stored tightly wrapped in foil for 2 days to mellow. To serve, place in 350°F (175°C) oven for 10 minutes or until heated through. Good cold too. Makes 1 loaf.

Pictured on cover.

❸

❹

Pumpernickel

Dark in color, coarse in texture, good in flavor.

500 mL	2 cups	Sunny Boy cereal (see Note)
250 mL	1 cup	All-purpose flour
5 mL	1 tsp.	Baking powder
5 mL	1 tsp.	Baking soda
5 mL	1 tsp.	Salt
500 mL	2 cups	Warm water
60 mL	¼ cup	Molasses

Combine first 5 ingredients in bowl. Stir. Make a well.

Stir water and molasses in small bowl. Pour into well. Stir to moisten. Batter will be quite runny. Turn into greased 9 x 5 inch (23 x 12 cm) loaf pan. Cover with foil. Bake in 300°F (150°C) oven for about 2 hours. Let stand 10 minutes before removing from pan. Yield: 1 loaf.

Pictured on this page.

Note: An uncooked raw cereal milled from wheat, rye and flax.

Cutting Board Courtesy Of:
Stokes

Whipped Cream Cake

This delicate pale yellow-colored cake has an excellent flavor and a moist fine texture.

250 mL	1 cup	Whipping cream	Beat cream in bowl until stiff.
2	2	Large eggs	Add eggs and vanilla. Beat until very light, about 2 minutes.
5 mL	1 tsp.	Vanilla	
250 mL	1 cup	Granulated sugar	Add sugar. Beat well.
425 mL	1¾ cups	All-purpose flour	Add flour, baking powder and salt. Beat until mixed. Turn into ungreased 10 inch (25 cm) angel food tube pan. Bake in 375°F (190°C) oven for 25 to 35 minutes until an inserted wooden pick comes out clean. Cool for 20 minutes before removing from pan. Will only rise half way up pan. Top with Vanilla Glaze. Yield: 1 cake.
10 mL	2 tsp.	Baking powder	
2 mL	½ tsp.	Salt	

Pictured on page 25.

Vanilla Glaze

250 mL	1 cup	Icing (confectioner's) sugar	Stir all ingredients together well. Add more icing sugar or water to make a barely pourable glaze. Drizzle over cake.
15 mL	1 tbsp.	Water	
1 mL	¼ tsp.	Vanilla	

Blueberry Coffee Cake

If berries are moist, you may want to coat them with a little of the flour before folding in. A go-with for coffee.

60 mL	¼ cup	Butter or hard margarine, softened	Cream butter and sugar well. Beat in egg. Add vanilla and milk. Mix.
175 mL	¾ cup	Granulated sugar	
1	1	Large egg	
5 mL	1 tsp.	Vanilla	
175 mL	¾ cup	Milk	
450 mL	2 cups	All-purpose flour	Add flour, baking powder and salt. Stir to moisten. Batter will be stiff.
15 mL	1 tbsp.	Baking powder	
2 mL	½ tsp.	Salt	
375 mL	1½ cups	Blueberries, fresh or frozen	Fold in blueberries. Spread in greased 12 cup (2.7 L) bundt pan.

Topping

| 60 mL | ¼ cup | Brown sugar, packed | Mix sugar and cinnamon. Sprinkle over top. Bake in 350°F (175°C) oven for 40 to 50 minutes until an inserted wooden pick comes out clean. Serve warm or cold with or without Custard Sauce, below. Yield: 1 cake. |
| 5 mL | 1 tsp. | Cinnamon | |

Custard Sauce

15 mL	1 tbsp.	Custard powder	Stir custard powder and sugar together well in saucepan. Mix in milk and vanilla. Heat and stir until it boils and thickens. Spoon over or around each serving. Makes 1 cup (225 mL).
15 mL	1 tbsp.	Granulated sugar	
225 mL	1 cup	Milk	
2 mL	½ tsp.	Vanilla	

Pictured on page 25.

Ginger Chiffon Cake

This makes a light-colored, lightly-flavored large cake.

450 mL	2 cups	Sifted cake flour
350 mL	1½ cups	Granulated sugar
15 mL	1 tbsp.	Baking powder
5 mL	1 tsp.	Salt
7 mL	1½ tsp.	Ginger
2 mL	½ tsp.	Cinnamon
1 mL	¼ tsp.	Cloves

Sift first 7 ingredients into medium mixing bowl. Make a well in center.

125 mL	½ cup	Cooking oil
7	7	Egg yolks (large)
125 mL	½ cup	Water
50 mL	¼ cup	Molasses

Add next 4 ingredients to well. Set aside. Don't beat yet.

7	7	Egg whites (large), room temperature
2 mL	½ tsp.	Cream of tartar

Beat egg whites and cream of tartar together in large mixing bowl until very stiff. Set aside. Using same beaters, beat egg yolk-flour mixture until smooth and light. Fold into beaten egg whites in about 4 or 5 additions. Pour into ungreased 10 inch (25 cm) angel food tube pan. Bake in 325°F (160°C) oven for 55 minutes. Increase heat to 350°F (175°C) and bake 10 to 15 minutes more until an inserted wooden pick comes out clean. Invert pan to cool. Vanilla Glaze, page 15, finishes this nicely. Yield: 1 cake.

Plate Courtesy Of:
Reed's China And Gift Shop

Chocolate Carrot Cake *Very moist. A good keeper.*

250 mL	1 cup	Cooking oil
425 mL	1¾ cups	Granulated sugar
4	4	Large eggs
125 mL	½ cup	Cocoa
500 mL	2 cups	Grated carrot
540 mL	19 oz.	Crushed pineapple, drained

Beat cooking oil and sugar in mixing bowl. Beat in eggs 1 at a time. Mix in cocoa. Stir in carrot and pineapple.

500 mL	2 cups	All-purpose flour
15 mL	1 tbsp.	Cinnamon
		Nutmeg, just a pinch
		Cloves, just a pinch
10 mL	2 tsp.	Baking powder
5 mL	1 tsp.	Baking soda
125 mL	½ cup	Chopped walnuts (optional)

Stir next 7 ingredients together in bowl. Add to batter. Stir. Turn into greased and floured 12 cup (2.7 L) bundt pan. Bake in 350°F (175°C) oven for 45 to 50 minutes until an inserted wooden pick comes out clean. Let stand for 15 minutes. Turn out onto rack. Cool. Yield: 1 cake.

Chocolate Cheese Icing

62 g	2 oz.	Cream cheese, softened
125 mL	½ cup	Icing (confectioner's) sugar
15 mL	1 tbsp.	Butter or hard margarine, softened
30 mL	2 tbsp.	Cocoa
0.5 mL	⅛ tsp.	Cinnamon
1 mL	¼ tsp.	Vanilla

Beat cream cheese, icing sugar and butter together until smooth. Add cocoa, cinnamon and vanilla. Mix slowly at first. Beat until smooth and creamy. Ice top of cake allowing some to go down sides.

Pictured on page 25.

Hawaiian Cake

This filling and topping will transform a mix or your favorite white cake into something special. Sometimes referred to as "Better Than Sex Cake".

1	1	Yellow cake mix, 2 layer size	Prepare cake mix according to package directions. Pour batter into three greased 9 inch (22 cm) layer pans or greased 10 inch (25 cm) angel food tube pan. Bake about 20 minutes in layer pans or about 45 minutes in tube pan, until an inserted wooden pick comes out clean. Cool.
540 mL	19 oz.	Chilled crushed pineapple, with juice	Mix pineapple with juice and pudding mix. Fold in topping. Chill until stiff enough to spread. Spread filling between layers and on sides and top. A tube cake can be sliced to make 3 layers and filled with same filling.
1	1	Large vanilla instant pudding, 6 serving size	
1 L	4 cups	Frozen non-dairy whipped topping, thawed	
30-50 mL	2-3 tbsp.	Chopped macadamia nuts or other	Sprinkle with nuts, cherries and coconut. Keep chilled. Yield: 1 triple layer cake.
30-50 mL	2-3 tbsp.	Chopped maraschino cherries	
30-50 mL	2-3 tbsp.	Shredded or flaked coconut	

Pictured on cover.

Variation: Use 15 oz. frozen sliced strawberries in syrup, thawed, in place of pineapple.

Orange Coffee Cake

Serve fresh and warm for a splendid snack.

60 mL	¼ cup	Butter or hard margarine, softened	Cream butter and sugar well. Beat in eggs 1 at a time. Add vanilla, orange rind and juice. Stir.
125 mL	½ cup	Granulated sugar	
2	2	Large eggs	
5 mL	1 tsp.	Vanilla	
30 mL	2 tbsp.	Grated orange rind	
200 mL	¾ cup	Orange juice from 1 orange plus water	
500 mL	2 cups	All-purpose flour	Add flour, baking powder and salt. Stir to moisten. Turn into greased 9 x 9 inch (22 x 22 cm) pan.
15 mL	1 tbsp.	Baking Powder	
2 mL	½ tsp.	Salt	

Topping

50 mL	3 tbsp.	Butter or hard margarine	Melt butter in small saucepan. Stir in sugar, flour and cinnamon. Sprinkle over top. Bake in 375°F (190°C) oven for 25 to 30 minutes or until an inserted wooden pick comes out clean. Serve warm. Cuts into 9 to 12 pieces.
75 mL	⅓ cup	Brown sugar, packed	
60 mL	¼ cup	All-purpose flour	
5 mL	1 tsp.	Cinnamon	

Pictured on page 25.

Rum Cake

Wonderful flavor to this golden crusted cake. A pound cake texture.

225 mL	1 cup	Butter or hard margarine, softened
400 mL	1¾ cups	Granulated sugar
4	4	Large eggs
5 mL	1 tsp.	Rum flavoring (see Note)

Cream butter and sugar together in mixing bowl. Beat in eggs 1 at a time. Add rum flavoring. Stir.

675 mL	3 cups	All-purpose flour
2 mL	½ tsp.	Baking powder
2 mL	½ tsp.	Baking soda
2 mL	½ tsp.	Salt

Combine flour, baking powder, baking soda and salt in medium bowl. Stir.

| 225 mL | 1 cup | Buttermilk |

Pictured below.

Add flour mixture alternately with buttermilk beginning and ending with flour. Pour into greased 10 inch (25 cm) angel food tube pan. Bake in 325°F (160°C) oven for about 1¼ hours or until an inserted wooden pick comes out clean. Yield: 1 cake.

Note: To use rum, omit rum flavoring. Replace ¼ of the buttermilk with rum.

Orange Chocolate Cake
A large extravagant cake with a chocolate-orange tunnel inside.

125 mL	½ cup	Butter or hard margarine, softened	Cream butter and sugar together well. Beat in egg yolks 1 at a time. Add vanilla.
450 mL	2 cups	Granulated sugar	
4	4	Egg yolks (large)	
5 mL	1 tsp.	Vanilla	
225 mL	1 cup	Hot mashed potatoes	Stir potatoes into first amount of milk. Add. Mix.
125 mL	½ cup	Milk	
450 mL	2 cups	Sifted cake flour	Stir flour, baking soda and cocoa together. Stir flour mixture in 3 parts alternately with second amount of milk in 2 parts, beginning and ending with flour.
15 mL	1 tbsp.	Baking soda	
125 mL	½ cup	Cocoa	
150 mL	⅔ cup	Milk	
4	4	Egg whites (large), room temperature	Beat egg whites until stiff. Fold in. Pour ¾ batter into greased and floured 12 cup (2.7 L) bundt pan.

Filling

350 mL	1½ cups	Semisweet chocolate chips	Stir all 4 ingredients together well. Spoon over top of batter, keeping it in center without touching sides. Spoon remaining batter over top. Bake in 350°F (175°C) oven for 60 to 70 minutes or until an inserted wooden pick comes out clean. Let stand 20 minutes before turning out onto plate. Cool. Yield: 1 cake.
175 mL	¾ cup	Chopped walnuts	
125 mL	½ cup	Sweetened condensed milk	
50 mL	3 tbsp.	Finely grated orange peel	

Continued on next page.

Orange Glaze

250 mL	1 cup	Icing (confectioner's) sugar
15 mL	1 tbsp.	Butter or hard margarine, softened
10 mL	2 tsp.	Finely grated orange rind
15 mL	1 tbsp.	Prepared orange juice

Mix all 4 ingredients until smooth, adding more or less orange juice as needed to make glaze barely pourable. Spoon over cake.

Pictured on cover.

Vanilla Wafer Cake

This has a custardy top. It will remind you of bread pudding. For variety, serve it warm with your favorite pudding sauce.

250 mL	1 cup	Butter or hard margarine, softened
500 mL	2 cups	Granulated sugar
6	6	Large eggs
125 mL	½ cup	Milk

Cream butter and sugar together well. Beat in eggs 1 at a time. Mix in milk.

341 g	12 oz.	Box of vanilla wafers, crushed into crumbs by rolling with rolling pin
250 mL	1 cup	Shredded coconut (or use flaked)
250 mL	1 cup	Chopped pecans

Stir in remaining ingredients. Turn into greased 10 inch (25 cm) angle food tube pan. Bake in 350°F (175°C) oven for about 45 minutes. Cool thoroughly in pan before turning out onto plate. May also be reheated and served warm. Yield: 1 cake.

Pictured on page 25.

Fruited Coffee Cake

A tasty change from traditional coffee cake.

1	1	Large egg	Beat egg, sugar and butter together well.
175 mL	¾ cup	Granulated sugar	
125 mL	½ cup	Butter or hard margarine, softened	
375 mL	1½ cups	All-purpose flour	Stir flour, baking powder and salt in small bowl.
10 mL	2 tsp.	Baking powder	
2 mL	½ tsp.	Salt	
125 mL	½ cup	Milk	Add flour mixture in 3 parts and milk in 2 parts, stirring to moisten.
60 mL	¼ cup	Cut glazed mixed fruit	Fold in glazed fruit, currants and raisins. Turn into greased 9 x 9 inch (22 x 22 cm) pan.
60 mL	¼ cup	Currants	
60 mL	¼ cup	Raisins	
60 mL	¼ cup	Brown sugar, packed	Mix brown sugar and cinnamon. Sprinkle over top. Bake in 350°F (175°C) oven for 25 to 30 minutes or until an inserted wooden pick comes out clean. Cuts into 9 to 12 pieces.
2 mL	½ tsp.	Cinnamon	

Pictured on page 25.

Snow Drops

Such delicate morsels. A melt-in-your mouth treat.

250 mL	1 cup	Butter or hard margarine, softened	Combine butter, icing sugar and vanilla in bowl. Beat until very creamy.
125 mL	½ cup	Icing (confectioner's) sugar	
10 mL	2 tsp.	Vanilla	
525 mL	2⅛ cups	Sifted cake flour	Mix in flour and walnuts. Chill until firm enough to be shaped. Form into the shape of a date. Arrange on baking sheet. Bake in 400°F (205°C) oven for 10 to 12 minutes.
250 mL	1 cup	Finely chopped walnuts	
75mL	⅓ cup	Icing (confectioner's) sugar, for coating	Roll in icing sugar while hot. Makes 40.

Pictured on cover.

Soft Ginger Cookies page 27

Soft Ginger Cookies

Think of picnics, lunch boxes, snacking. These are good for anything.

1	1	Large egg	Using large bowl, beat egg until frothy. Add melted butter, sugar, molasses and milk. Mix.
125 mL	½ cup	Butter or hard margarine, melted	
125 mL	½ cup	Granulated sugar	
250 mL	1 cup	Mild molasses	
125 mL	½ cup	Cold milk	
375 mL	1½ cups	All-purpose flour	In separate bowl place next 6 ingredients. Stir well. Add to first bowl. Mix.
2 mL	½ tsp.	Baking soda	
15 mL	1 tbsp.	Baking powder	
7 mL	1½ tsp.	Ginger	
7 mL	1½ tsp.	Cinnamon	
4 mL	¾ tsp.	Salt	
675 mL	2¾ cups	All-purpose flour	Add remaining flour. Stir to combine. Chill ½ hour. Roll ½ inch (12 cm) thick on a lightly floured surface. Cut into 2 inch (5 cm) rounds. Arrange on ungreased baking sheet allowing room for expansion. Bake in 400°F (205°C) oven for 10 to 12 minutes. Yield: 45 cookies.

Pictured on page 26.

China Courtesy Of:
Reed's China And Gift Shop

Coconut Cookies

A thin cookie base topped with a chewy coconut cap.

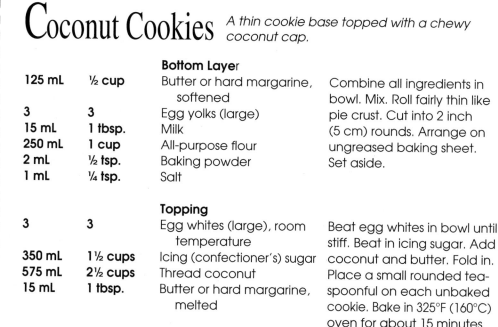

Bottom Layer

125 mL	½ cup	Butter or hard margarine, softened
3	3	Egg yolks (large)
15 mL	1 tbsp.	Milk
250 mL	1 cup	All-purpose flour
2 mL	½ tsp.	Baking powder
1 mL	¼ tsp.	Salt

Combine all ingredients in bowl. Mix. Roll fairly thin like pie crust. Cut into 2 inch (5 cm) rounds. Arrange on ungreased baking sheet. Set aside.

Topping

3	3	Egg whites (large), room temperature
350 mL	1½ cups	Icing (confectioner's) sugar
575 mL	2½ cups	Thread coconut
15 mL	1 tbsp.	Butter or hard margarine, melted

Beat egg whites in bowl until stiff. Beat in icing sugar. Add coconut and butter. Fold in. Place a small rounded teaspoonful on each unbaked cookie. Bake in 325°F (160°C) oven for about 15 minutes until light brown. Makes about 4 dozen cookies.

Pictured on page 65.

Fruitcake Cookies

Mildly spiced, heavily fruited. A special-time cookie.

450 mL	2 cups	Candied cut mixed fruit	Measure first 5 ingredients into bowl. Stir to coat fruit with flour. Set aside.
225 mL	1 cup	Raisins	
225 mL	1 cup	Chopped dates	
225 mL	1 cup	Chopped pecans	
125 mL	½ cup	All-purpose flour	
125 mL	½ cup	Butter or hard margarine, softened	Cream butter and sugar together. Beat in eggs 1 at a time. Add vanilla.
225 mL	1 cup	Granulated sugar	
2	2	Large eggs	
5 mL	1 tsp.	Vanilla	
450 mL	1 cup	All-purpose flour	Stir second amount of flour, baking soda and cinnamon together and add. Mix. Stir in floured fruit. Drop by tea-spoonfuls onto greased baking sheet. Bake in 325°F (160°C) oven for 15 to 18 minutes. Makes about 6 dozen cookies.
2 mL	½ tsp.	Baking soda	
1 mL	¼ tsp.	Cinnamon (optional)	

Pictured on cover.

Cherry Snacks

Excellent flavor. A soft and moist drop cookie.

250 mL	1 cup	Butter or hard margarine, softened	Mix first 4 ingredients in bowl.
175 mL	¾ cup	Granulated sugar	
500 mL	2 cups	All-purpose flour	
2 mL	½ tsp.	Salt	
5 mL	1 tsp.	Baking soda	Stir baking soda into water.
60 mL	¼ cup	Boiling water	Add. Mix.
250 mL	1 cup	Chopped dates	Add remaining ingredients.
250 mL	1 cup	Chopped walnuts	Stir to distribute evenly. Drop
250 mL	1 cup	Chopped glazed cherries	by large teaspoonfuls onto
175 mL	¾ cup	Medium coconut	greased baking sheet. Bake in 350°F (175°C) oven for about 15 minutes. Yield: 4 dozen cookies.

Pictured on page 65.

Walnut Chews

Chocolate Shortbrea

Walnut Chews

Quick, economical and chewy.

125 mL	½ cup	Butter or hard margarine, softened	Cream butter and sugar together well. Beat in egg and vanilla until fluffy.
375 mL	1½ cups	Brown sugar, packed	
1	1	Large egg	
5 mL	1 tsp.	Vanilla	
375 mL	1½ cups	All-purpose flour	Stir in flour, baking powder and walnuts. Drop by teaspoon-fuls onto greased cookie sheet. Bake in 350°F (175°C) oven for 12 to 15 minutes. Yield: 40 cookies.
2 mL	½ tsp.	Baking powder	
125 mL	½ cup	Chopped walnuts	

Pictured on page 30.

Chocolate Shortbread

So crisp and tender. For a variation, top each with a piece of glazed or maraschino cherry.

425 mL	1¾ cups	All-purpose flour	Combine all ingredients in bowl. Mix as for pie crust. Shape into 2 rolls. Chill. Slice ¼ inch (6 mm) thick and arrange on ungreased baking sheet. If you prefer, roll on lightly floured surface ¼ inch (6 mm) thick. Cut into fancy shapes. Arrange on ungreased baking sheet. Bake in 325°F (160°C) oven for about 12 to 15 minutes. Yield: 45 cookies.
125 mL	½ cup	Icing (confectioner's) sugar	
60 mL	¼ cup	Cocoa	
250 mL	1 cup	Butter, softened (not margarine)	

Pictured on page 30.

Heavenly Clouds

The peanut brittle dissolves in the whipped cream to transform this into the title.

4	4	Egg whites (large), room temperature	Combine first 6 ingredients in bowl. Beat until soft peaks form.
5 mL	1 tsp.	Vanilla	
5 mL	1 tsp.	White vinegar	
5 mL	1 tsp.	Water	
2 mL	½ tsp.	Baking Powder	
1 mL	¼ tsp.	Salt	
275 mL	1¼ cups	Granulated sugar (berry sugar is best)	While continuing to beat add sugar gradually, beating until stiff. Outline 2 circles on foil, each about 9 inches (22 cm) in diameter. Place foil on baking sheet. Grease circles. Spread ½ meringue on each circle. Bake in 150°F (65°C) oven for 1½ hours. Cool. Carefully remove foil. Can be stored in dry place until next day.

Filling

500 mL	2 cups	Whipping cream (or 2 envelopes topping)	Beat cream in small mixing bowl until stiff. Fold in crushed peanut brittle. Spread ½ filling over 1 meringue layer. Cover with second layer. Spread remaining ½ filling over top. Chill at least 3 hours before serving. Freezes well. Cuts into 6 to 8 wedges.
230 g	8 oz.	Finely crushed peanut brittle (use blender or grinder)	

Lemon Meringues

Add a dab of whipped cream to complete this superb dessert.

Meringues

Metric	Imperial	Ingredient	Instructions
4	4	Egg whites (large), room temperature	Beat egg whites in mixing bowl until soft peaks form.
225 mL	1 cup	Granulated sugar	Gradually beat in sugar.
5 mL	1 tsp.	Baking powder	Add remaining ingredients. Beat in. Line 2 baking sheets with foil. Divide meringue into 5 to 6 dollops on each sheet. Press into 4 inch (10 cm) circles making dip in center with higher sides. Bake in 275°F (140°C) oven for 1 hour. Turn off heat. Allow to cool in oven at least 1 hour with oven door slightly ajar.
0.5 mL	⅛ tsp.	Salt	
5 mL	1 tsp.	White vinegar	
5 mL	1 tsp.	Vanilla	

Lemon Filling

Metric	Imperial	Ingredient	Instructions
450 mL	2 cups	Water	Bring water to a boil in saucepan.
225 mL	1 cup	Granulated sugar	Mix next 6 ingredients in bowl in order given. Stir into water until it returns to a boil and thickens. Cool. Divide among shells. Bottom center is more tender if filled 2 hours or more before serving. Do not freeze. Serves 10 to 12.
75 mL	5 tbsp.	Cornstarch	
10 mL	2 tsp.	Grated lemon rind	
75 mL	⅓ cup	Lemon juice	
4	4	Egg yolks (large)	
1 mL	¼ tsp.	Salt	

Pompadour Pudding

So different. A chocolate layer covers a vanilla custard sauce. Excellent.

2	2	Egg yolks (large)	Beat egg yolks with spoon in saucepan. Stir in sugar, salt and milk. Stir. Add cornstarch and vanilla. Heat and stir until it boils and thickens. Pour into 1 quart (1 L) casserole.
75 mL	⅓ cup	Granulated sugar	
1 mL	¼ tsp.	Salt	
450 mL	2 cups	Milk	
30 mL	2 tbsp.	Cornstarch	
5 mL	1 tsp.	Vanilla	

Topping

1 x 28 g	1 x 1 oz.	Unsweetened chocolate baking square	Cut chocolate into small pieces. Melt in heavy saucepan over low heat. Stir often. Remove from heat.
75 mL	⅓ cup	Granulated sugar	Stir in sugar and milk. If mixture is warm cool to room temperature.
30 mL	2 tbsp.	Milk	
2	2	Egg whites (large), room temperature	Beat egg whites in small mixing bowl until stiff. Fold into chocolate mixture. Spread over pudding. Bake in 375°F (190°C) oven for about 20 minutes or until top feels dry and firm. Do not freeze. Makes 4 to 6 servings.

Pictured on cover.

Apple Pie Dessert

Actually a cake baked in a pie plate. Serve warm with ice cream or cold with whipped cream.

60 mL	¼ cup	Butter or hard margarine, softened
250 mL	1 cup	Granulated sugar
1	1	Large egg
5 mL	1 tsp.	Vanilla
30 mL	2 tbsp.	Hot water

Cream butter and sugar well in mixing bowl. Beat in egg, vanilla and hot water.

250 mL	1 cup	All-purpose flour
5 mL	1 tsp.	Baking soda
5 mL	1 tsp.	Cinnamon
2 mL	½ tsp.	Nutmeg
1 mL	¼ tsp.	Salt

Stir in next 5 ingredients.

625 mL	2½ cups	Peeled and diced cooking apples (McIntosh is good)
125 mL	½ cup	Chopped walnuts
125 mL	½ cup	Raisins

Add apples, nuts and raisins. Stir. Turn into greased 9 inch (22 cm) pie plate. Bake in 350°F (175°C) oven for about 40 minutes or until an inserted wooden pick comes out clean. Serve warm. May also be served cold. Cuts into 6 or 8 wedges.

Pictured on this page.

Plate Courtesy Of:
Reed's China And Gift Shop

Cappuccino Cheesecake

Indulge in this impressive dessert. Freezes well.

Crust

75 mL	⅓ cup	Butter or hard margarine
300 mL	1⅓ cups	Graham cracker crumbs
75 mL	⅓ cup	Granulated sugar
50 mL	3 tbsp.	Cocoa

Melt butter in small saucepan. Stir in crumbs, sugar and cocoa. Press into 9 inch (22 cm) springform pan. Set aside.

Filling

3 x 250 g	3 x 8 oz.	Cream cheese, softened
125 mL	½ cup	Brown sugar, packed
125 mL	½ cup	Granulated sugar
30 mL	2 tbsp.	All-purpose flour
10 mL	2 tsp.	Coffee liqueur (or vanilla)
3	3	Large eggs, room temperature

Beat cream cheese, both sugars, flour and liqueur together well. Beat in eggs 1 at a time, beating only until mixed in.

60 mL	¼ cup	Milk
15 mL	1 tbsp.	Instant coffee granules

Combine milk and coffee granules in cup. Stir until coffee is completely dissolved. Mix into batter in bowl. Turn into prepared pan. Bake in 300°F (150°C) oven for about 1½ hours until center is still a bit wobbly when pan is gently shaken. Run knife around sides of pan to loosen cake. This will help prevent cracks. Place pan on rack to cool. Cover lightly with waxed paper and chill all day or overnight before serving.

Continued on next page.

Topping

125 mL	½ cup	Whipping cream (or ½ envelope topping)	Beat whipping cream, sugar and vanilla in small bowl until stiff. Place small dollops over top. Garnish with shaved chocolate. Cuts into 12 wedges.
2 mL	½ tsp.	Granulated sugar	
1 mL	¼ tsp.	Vanilla	
		Shaved chocolate for garnish	

Pictured on page 41.

Caramel Apple Crisp
Serve warm with ice cream for an unbelievable comfort dessert.

16	16	Caramels, light brown, 3½ oz. (100 g)	Put caramels, reserved apple syrup and lemon juice in large saucepan. Heat and stir until melted and smooth.
60 mL	¼ cup	Reserved syrup from apples	
15 mL	1 tbsp.	Lemon juice, fresh or bottled	
3 x 398 mL	3 x 14 oz.	Canned sliced apples in syrup, drained, syrup reserved (see Note)	Add apple slices. Stir. Turn into 2 quart (2 L) casserole.

Topping

75 mL	⅓ cup	All-purpose flour	Mix all ingredients together until crumbly. Sprinkle over top. Bake in 375°F (190°C) oven for about 35 minutes. Makes 8 servings.
60 mL	¼ cup	Granulated sugar	
1 mL	¼ tsp.	Cinnamon	
30 mL	2 tbsp.	Butter or hard margarine, softened	

Note: To use fresh apples, cook 4½ cups (1 L) peeled, sliced cooking apples (McIntosh is good) with ¼ cup (60 mL) water and ½ cup (125 mL) brown sugar until tender crisp.

Brownie Ice Cream Cake

When reaching into the freezer for this dessert, you may find it has vanished.

First Layer

175 mL	¾ cup	Granulated sugar
125 mL	½ cup	All-purpose flour
125 mL	½ cup	Cocoa
2 mL	½ tsp.	Baking powder
1 mL	¼ tsp.	Salt
2	2	Large eggs
125 mL	½ cup	Butter or hard margarine, softened
2 mL	½ tsp.	Vanilla

Measure all ingredients into mixing bowl. Beat at medium-low speed until smooth. Pour into greased 9 inch (22 cm) springform pan. Bake in 350°F (175°C) oven for 25 to 30 minutes until an inserted wooden pick comes out clean but moist. Cool.

Second Layer

250 g	8 oz.	Cream cheese, softened
60 mL	¼ cup	Corn syrup
1 L	4 cups	Vanilla ice cream, softened slightly

Beat cream cheese and corn syrup together. Slowly beat in ice cream. Spread ½ mixture over cooled first layer.

75 mL	⅓ cup	Chocolate sundae topping

Drizzle with sundae topping. Cover with second ½ ice cream mixture. Cover. Freeze.

Third layer

150 mL	⅔ cup	Chocolate sundae topping

Drizzle sundae topping over top. Let stand about 10 minutes. Cuts into 10 to 12 wedges.

Chocolate Amaretto Cheesecake

Garnish with amaretto flavored whipped cream for a more lavish dessert.

Crust

60 mL	¼ cup	Butter or hard margarine	
50 mL	3 tbsp.	Granulated sugar	
275 mL	1¼ cups	Graham cracker crumbs	
50 mL	3 tbsp.	Cocoa	

Melt butter in saucepan. Stir in sugar, crumbs and cocoa. Press into ungreased 9 inch (22 cm) springform pan. Chill.

Filling

2 x 250 g	2 x 8 oz.	Cream cheese, softened
125 mL	½ cup	Granulated sugar
2	2	Large eggs
6 x 28 g	6 x 1 oz.	Semisweet chocolate baking squares, chopped, melted and cooled
150 mL	⅔ cup	Sour cream
75 mL	⅓ cup	Amaretto liqueur
5 mL	1 tsp.	Vanilla
2 mL	½ tsp.	Almond Flavoring

Beat cream cheese and sugar well. Beat in eggs 1 at a time until just blended. Stir in next 5 ingredients. Bake in 300°F (150°C) oven for 1 hour. Turn oven off. Do not open oven door. Leave cheesecake in oven for 1 more hour. Cool, then chill overnight.

Topping

2 x 28 g	2 x 1 oz.	Semisweet chocolate baking squares, chopped
5 mL	1 tsp.	Butter or hard margarine
28-30	28-30	Whole almonds

Heat and stir chocolate and butter in top of double boiler until smooth. Dip ends of almonds in chocolate. Chill on waxed paper. Arrange in pattern on top. Cuts into 8 to 10 wedges.

Pictured on cover.

Bavarian Apple Torte *Fabulous and different.*

Crust

125 mL	½ cup	Butter or hard margarine, softened	Cream butter and sugar together well in bowl. Mix in flour. Press in bottom and half way up sides of 9 inch (22 cm) springform pan.
75 mL	⅓ cup	Granulated sugar	
250 mL	1 cup	All-purpose flour	

Filling

125 mL	½ cup	Raspberry jam	Spread jam over crust.
250 g	8 oz.	Cream cheese, softened	Beat cream cheese and sugar together well. Beat in egg and vanilla until just blended. Pour over jam.
60 mL	¼ cup	Granulated sugar	
1	1	Large egg	
2 mL	½ tsp.	Vanilla	

Topping

75 mL	⅓ cup	Granulated sugar	Stir sugar and cinnamon together in large bowl. Add apples. Toss to coat. Arrange over cheese mixture.
2 mL	½ tsp.	Cinnamon	
1 L	4 cups	Peeled, thinly sliced cooking apples (McIntosh is good)	
60 mL	¼ cup	Sliced almonds, toasted in 350°F (175°) oven	Sprinkle with toasted almonds. Bake in 450°F (230°C) oven for 10 minutes. Reduce heat to 400°F (205°C). Continue to bake for about 25 minutes until apples are tender. Place pan on rack. Run knife around edge to loosen. Let stand for 30 minutes before removing from pan. Serve either warm or room temperature. May be reheated in 350°F (175°C) oven for 10 to 12 minutes. Do not freeze. Cuts into 10 to 12 wedges.

1. Cappuccino Cheesecake page 36
2. Bavarian Apple Torte page 40
3. Mock Mince Pie page 59

China Courtesy Of:
Reed's China And Gift Shop

Gold Cake Server Courtesy Of:
The Royal Doulton Store

Pictured on page 41.

Brazil Loaf

This is a solid nutty loaf with cherries adding the color.

675 mL	3 cups	Whole Brazil nuts	Place first 3 ingredients in bowl.
500 mL	2¼ cups	Glazed cherries	
4	4	Glazed pineapple rings, cubed	
275 mL	1¼ cups	All-purpose flour	Mix flour, sugar, baking powder and salt together. Add to fruit. Stir thoroughly to coat.
175 mL	¾ cup	Granulated sugar	
5 mL	1 tsp.	Baking powder	
2 mL	½ tsp.	Salt	
3	3	Large eggs	Beat eggs in small mixing bowl until frothy. Add butter, vanilla and almond flavoring. Mix. Pour over fruit mixture. Stir until moistened. Turn into 9 x 5 inch (23 x 12 cm) loaf pan lined with greased brown paper. Press down. Bake in 300°F (150°C) oven for about 1¾ to 2 hours until an inserted wooden pick comes out clean. Let stand 20 minutes. Remove from pan to rack. Cool. Discard brown paper. Wrap with plastic. Yield: 1 loaf.
125 mL	½ cup	Butter or hard margarine, softened	
5 mL	1 tsp.	Vanilla	
5 mL	1 tsp.	Almond flavoring	

Pictured on page 11.

Tropical Loaf
Incredibly delicious and attractive.

2	2	Large eggs	Beat eggs in bowl until frothy. Beat in sugar. Stir in next 6 ingredients.
175 mL	¾ cup	Granulated sugar	
125 mL	½ cup	Cooking oil	
250 mL	1 cup	Mashed banana	
398 mL	14 oz.	Crushed pineapple, drained	
5 mL	1 tsp.	Vanilla	
150 mL	⅔ cup	Maraschino cherries, drained and halved	
125 mL	½ cup	Chopped pecans (or walnuts)	
425 mL	1¾ cups	All-purpose flour	Add remaining ingredients. Stir to moisten. Turn into greased 9 x 5 inch (23 x 12 cm) loaf pan. Bake in 350°F (175°C) oven for 60 to 70 minutes until an inserted wooden pick comes out clean. Let stand 10 minutes. Turn out onto rack. Cool and wrap with plastic. Yield: 1 loaf.
2 mL	½ tsp.	Baking soda	
2 mL	½ tsp.	Baking powder	
2 mL	½ tsp.	Salt	

Pictured on page 49.

Pineapple Nut Loaf

Not just a bran loaf. The flavor is more than healthy.

60 mL	¼ cup	Cooking oil
175 mL	¾ cup	Brown sugar, packed
1	1	Large egg
5 mL	1 tsp.	Vanilla
398 mL	14 oz.	Crushed pineapple
500 mL	2¼ cups	All-purpose flour
15 mL	1 tbsp.	Baking powder
2 mL	½ tsp.	Baking soda
2 mL	½ tsp.	Salt
225 mL	1 cup	Natural bran
125 mL	½ cup	Chopped walnuts

Mix cooking oil, sugar and egg in bowl.

Stir in vanilla and pineapple.

Add remaining ingredients. Stir to moisten. Turn into greased 9 x 5 inch (23 x 12 cm) loaf pan. Bake in 350°F (175°C) oven for about 1 hour until an inserted wooden pick comes out clean. Let stand 10 minutes before removing from pan. Cool and wrap with plastic. Yield: 1 loaf.

Pictured below.

Cherry Bran Loaf *A cherry almond flavor. A pretty loaf.*

60 mL	¼ cup	Butter or hard margarine, softened	Cream butter and sugar in mixing bowl. Beat in egg. Add milk and flavoring. Stir.
175 mL	¾ cup	Granulated sugar	
1	1	Large egg	
225 mL	1 cup	Milk	
2 mL	½ tsp.	Almond flavoring	
450 mL	2 cups	All-purpose flour	Add next 4 ingredients. Stir until moistened.
225 mL	1 cup	All-bran cereal (100%)	
15 mL	1 tbsp.	Baking powder	
5 mL	1 tsp.	Salt	
150 mL	⅔ cup	Maraschino cherries, drained and chopped	Add cherries and walnuts. Stir enough to distribute. Turn into greased 9 x 5 inch (23 x 12 cm) loaf pan. Bake in 350°F (175°C) oven for 50 to 60 minutes until an inserted wooden pick comes out clean. Let stand for 10 minutes. Remove to rack. Cool and wrap with plastic. Yield: 1 loaf.
125 mL	½ cup	Chopped walnuts or pecans	

Pictured on cover.

Gumdrop Loaf
This bursts with color. Youngsters love it.

125 mL	½ cup	Butter or hard margarine, softened	Cream butter and sugar together well. Beat in eggs 1 at a time. Add vanilla.
250 mL	1 cup	Granulated sugar	
2	2	Large eggs	
5 mL	1 tsp.	Vanilla	
550 mL	2¼ cups	All-purpose flour	Stir flour, baking powder and salt together in separate bowl.
10 mL	2 tsp.	Baking powder	
1 mL	¼ tsp.	Salt	
250mL	1 cup	Milk	Add milk in 2 parts alternately with flour mixture in 3 parts, beginning and ending with flour.
500 g	1 lb.	Baking gums or regular gumdrops (no black), chopped	Stir in gumdrops and raisins. Turn into greased 9 x 5 inch (23 x 12 cm) loaf pan. Bake in 300°F (150°C) oven for about 2 hours until an inserted wooden pick comes out clean. Let stand 20 minutes before removing to rack. Cool and wrap with plastic. Yield: 1 loaf.
250 mL	1 cup	Raisins	

Pictured on cover.

Chocolate Mocha Loaf

This loaf has a rippled top like no other. A sprinkling of chocolate chips does the trick.

60 mL	¼ cup	Butter or hard margarine, softened	Cream butter and sugar in bowl. Beat in eggs 1 at a time. Stir in vanilla, milk and coffee granules.
250 mL	1 cup	Granulated sugar	
2	2	Large eggs	
5 mL	1 tsp.	Vanilla	
250 mL	1 cup	Milk	
15 mL	1 tbsp.	Instant coffee granules (optional)	
500 mL	2 cups	All-purpose flour	Stir next 4 ingredients together and add. Stir to moisten. Turn into greased 9 x 5 cm (23 x 12 cm) loaf pan.
125 mL	½ cup	Cocoa	
15 mL	1 tbsp.	Baking powder	
4 mL	¾ tsp.	Salt	
60 mL	¼ cup	Semisweet chocolate chips	Sprinkle with chocolate chips. Bake in 350°F (175°C) oven for about 1 hour until an inserted wooden pick comes out clean. Cool 10 minutes. Remove to rack. Cool completely and wrap with plastic. Yield: 1 loaf.

Pictured on page 48.

Strawberry Loaf

Use frozen berries to make this moist tasty loaf.

500 mL	2 cups	All-purpose flour	In large bowl thoroughly mix
250 mL	1 cup	Granulated sugar	first 5 ingredients. Make a
5 mL	1 tsp.	Cinnamon	well in center.
2 mL	½ tsp.	Baking soda	
2 mL	½ tsp.	Salt	
2	2	Large eggs	In small bowl beat eggs until
125 mL	½ cup	Cooking oil	frothy. Pour into well along
			with cooking oil.
425 g	15 oz.	Frozen sliced strawberries in syrup, thawed, drained, syrup reserved	Add strawberries, reserved syrup and pecans to well. Stir to combine. Turn into greased
125 mL	½ cup	Reserved strawberry syrup	9 x 5 inch (23 x 12 cm) loaf pan.
125 mL	½ cup	Chopped pecans (or walnuts)	Bake in 350°F (175°C) oven for about 1 hour or until an inserted toothpick comes out clean. Let stand 10 minutes. Turn out onto rack. Cool and wrap with plastic. Yield: 1 loaf.

Pictured below.

1. Chocolate Mocha Loaf page 47
2. Strawberry Loaf page 48
3. Tropical Loaf page 43
4. Pumpkin Loaf page 49

Pumpkin Loaf

Good flavor, good color and good size. A winner.

2	**2**	Large eggs	Beat eggs in mixing bowl until frothy. Add sugar, cooking oil, water and pumpkin. Beat well to mix.
275 mL	**1¼ cups**	Granulated sugar	
125 mL	**½ cup**	Cooking oil	
75 mL	**⅓ cup**	Water	
225 mL	**1 cup**	Canned pumpkin, without spices	

450 mL	**2 cups**	All-purpose flour	Add remaining ingredients. Stir until moistened. Turn into greased 9 x 5 inch (23 x 12 cm) pan. Bake in 350°F (175°C) oven for about 60 to 65 minutes until an inserted wooden pick comes out clean. Let stand 10 minutes. Remove from pan to rack. Cool and wrap with plastic. Yield: 1 loaf.
5 mL	**1 tsp.**	Baking soda	
2 mL	**½ tsp.**	Baking powder	
2 mL	**½ tsp.**	Salt	
5 mL	**1 tsp.**	Cinnamon	
4 mL	**¾ tsp.**	Nutmeg	
2 mL	**½ tsp.**	Allspice	
125 mL	**½ cup**	Chopped walnuts	
125 mL	**½ cup**	Raisins	

Pictured below.

Cranberry Orange Muffins

Good enough to be dessert.

500 mL	2 cups	All-purpose flour	Combine first 4 ingredients in bowl. Stir. Make a well.
125 mL	½ cup	Granulated sugar	
15 mL	1 tbsp.	Baking powder	
2 mL	½ tsp.	Salt	
2	2	Large eggs	Beat eggs with spoon in small bowl. Stir in butter, orange rind, orange juice and vanilla. Pour into well. Stir to moisten.
60 mL	¼ cup	Butter or hard margarine, melted	
1	1	Grated rind of orange	
250 mL	1 cup	Juice of orange plus water to make	
5 mL	1 tsp.	Vanilla	
250 mL	1 cup	Chopped cranberries, fresh or frozen, thawed	Blot cranberries with paper towel. Fold into batter. Fill greased medium muffin cups at least ¾ full. Bake in 400°F (205°C) oven for 15 to 20 minutes until an inserted wooden pick comes out clean. Yield: 12 muffins.

Pictured on cover.

Good Morning Muffins *Breakfast in a bite!*

6	6	Bacon slices	Cook bacon in frying pan until crispy. Cool and crumble. Reserve drippings.
60 mL	¼ cup	Reserved bacon fat plus cooking oil	Beat reserved fat and cooking oil with egg. Stir in milk.
1	1	Large egg	
250 mL	1 cup	Milk	
500 mL	2 cups	All-purpose flour	Add next 5 ingredients and bacon. Stir just to moisten. Fill greased medium muffin cups ¾ full.
15 mL	1 tbsp.	Baking powder	
15 mL	1 tbsp.	Granulated sugar	
2 mL	½ tsp.	Salt	
175 mL	¾ cup	Grated sharp (or medium) Cheddar cheese	
30 mL	2 tbsp.	Grated sharp (or medium) Cheddar cheese	Sprinkle with remaining cheese. Bake in 400°F (205°C) oven for 15 to 20 minutes until an inserted wooden pick comes out clean. Let stand 5 minutes. Remove to cool. Yield: 12 muffins.

Pictured on page 11.

Chocolate Bran Muffins

Yummy. Drizzle or ice with chocolate and serve with coffee or tea for a special treat.

75 mL	⅓ cup	Butter or hard margarine, softened	Cream butter and sugar together well. Beat in egg.
175 mL	¾ cup	Granulated sugar	
1	1	Large egg	
225 mL	1 cup	Milk	Stir milk and cereal together in small bowl. Let stand 10 minutes. Add to egg mixture.
225 mL	1 cup	All Bran cereal (100%)	
350 mL	1½ cups	All-purpose flour	Add remaining ingredients. Stir just to moisten. Fill greased medium muffin cups ¾ full. Bake in 400°F (205°C) oven for about 15 minutes until an inserted wooden pick comes out clean. Let stand 5 minutes. Remove to rack to cool. Yield: 12 muffins.
60 mL	¼ cup	Cocoa	
15 mL	1 tbsp.	Baking powder	
2 mL	½ tsp.	Salt	

❶

Pictured below.

Nutty Oat Muffins

Good nutty flavor. Nuts may be increased if desired.

75 mL	⅓ cup	Rolled oats (not instant)	Combine rolled oats and milk in bowl. Let stand 10 minutes.
200 mL	¾ cup	Milk	
125 mL	½ cup	Butter or hard margarine, softened	Cream butter and sugar in mixing bowl. Beat in eggs 1 at a time. Add vanilla and oat mixture. Stir.
75 mL	⅓ cup	Brown sugar, packed	
2	2	Large eggs	
2 mL	½ tsp.	Vanilla	
375 mL	1½ cups	All-purpose flour	Add flour, baking powder, salt and walnuts. Stir just to moisten. Fill greased medium muffin cups at least ¾ full. Bake in 400°F (205°C) oven about 15 to 20 minutes until an inserted wooden pick comes out clean. Let stand about 5 minutes before removing from pan. Yield: 12 muffins.
15 mL	1 tbsp.	Baking powder	
1 mL	¼ tsp.	Salt	
125 mL	½ cup	Chopped walnuts	

Pictured on this page.

1. **Chocolate Bran Muffins page 52**

2. **Nutty Oat Muffins page 53**

Fruity Oatmeal Muffins

So colorful with cranberries peeking through the top.

300 mL	1 ¼ cups	All-purpose flour	Combine first 6 ingredients in large bowl. Stir. Make a well in center.
250 mL	1 cup	Rolled oats (not instant)	
60 mL	¼ cup	Brown sugar, packed	
15 mL	1 tbsp.	Baking powder	
2 mL	½ tsp.	Salt	
1 mL	¼ tsp.	Cinnamon	
1	1	Large egg	In medium bowl, beat egg until frothy. Mix in honey, cooking oil, milk and vanilla.
30 mL	2 tbsp.	Honey	
60 mL	¼ cup	Cooking oil	
125 mL	½ cup	Milk	
5 mL	1 tsp.	Vanilla	
250 mL	1 cup	Cranberries, fresh or frozen, halved	Add cranberries and apples to egg mixture. Stir. Pour into well. Stir just to moisten. Fill greased medium muffin cups ¾ full. Bake in 400°F (205°C) oven for 15 to 20 minutes until an inserted wooden pick comes out clean. Let stand 5 minutes. Remove from pan. Yield: 12 muffins.
2	2	Cooking apples (McIntosh is good), peeled, cored and diced	

Pictured on page 11.

Blueberry Lemon Muffins *Exquisite flavor.*

60 mL	¼ cup	Butter or hard margarine, softened	Cream butter and sugar together well. Beat in egg. Add vanilla and milk. Stir.
75 mL	⅓ cup	Granulated sugar	
1	1	Large egg	
5 mL	1 tsp.	Vanilla	
250 mL	1 cup	Milk	

500 mL	2 cups	All-purpose flour	Add next 4 ingredients. Stir just to moisten.
10 mL	2 tsp.	Baking powder	
2 mL	½ tsp.	Salt	
1	1	Finely grated rind from lemon	

| 250 mL | 1 cup | Blueberries, fresh or frozen (don't thaw) | Quickly fold in blueberries. Fill greased medium muffin cups ¾ full. Bake in 400°F (205°C) oven for 15 to 20 minutes until an inserted wooden pick comes out clean. Let stand 5 minutes before removing from pan. |

Topping

| 1 | 1 | Juice of lemon | Stir lemon juice and sugar in small saucepan over medium heat until sugar dissolves. Brush over hot muffins. Makes 12. |
| 60 mL | ¼ cup | Granulated sugar | |

Pictured on page 11.

Tassies

Dainty little treats.

Cheese Pastry

125 mL	½ cup	Butter or hard margarine, softened
125 g	4 oz.	Cream cheese, softened
250 mL	1 cup	All-purpose flour

Cream butter, cream cheese and flour together well. Chill for 1 hour. Shape into long thin roll. Mark off, then cut into 24 pieces. Press into small tart tins, 1¾ inch (4.5 cm), to form shells.

Filling

1	1	Large egg
175 mL	¾ cup	Brown sugar, packed
15 mL	1 tbsp.	Butter or hard margarine, softened
5 mL	1 tsp.	Vanilla

Beat egg, brown sugar, butter and vanilla together well with spoon.

125 mL	½ cup	Chopped pecans (or walnuts)

Divide nuts among shells. Spoon mixture over top. Bake in 325°F (160°C) oven for about 25 minutes until filling is set. Makes 24 tassies.

Pictured on cover.

Sweet Pastry Pie

A thick tender crust holds a creamy almond filling. Quite a different method of preparation.

Sweet Pastry

60 mL	¼ cup	Butter or hard margarine, softened	Cream butter, sugar and egg together well.
60 mL	¼ cup	Granulated sugar	
1	1	Large egg	
225 mL	1 cup	All-purpose flour	Add flour, baking powder and salt. Mix and press into 9 inch (22 cm) pie plate. Bake in 350°F (175°C) oven for 8 to 10 minutes until golden.
5 mL	1 tsp.	Baking powder	
1 mL	¼ tsp.	Salt	

Filling

275 mL	1¼ cups	Milk	Heat milk in double boiler.
30 mL	2 tbsp.	All-purpose flour	Combine next 5 ingredients in small bowl. Stir well. Add to milk. Stir until thickened. Remove from heat.
50 mL	3 tbsp.	Granulated sugar	
2	2	Egg yolks (large)	
15 mL	1 tbsp.	Butter or hard margarine	
1 mL	¼ tsp.	Salt	
2 mL	½ tsp.	Vanilla	Stir in vanilla and almond flavoring.
2 mL	½ tsp.	Almond flavoring	
2	2	Egg whites (large), room temperature	Beat egg whites in small mixing bowl until stiff. Fold into hot mixture. Pour into pie shell. Bake in 350°F (175°C) oven for 15 minutes. Cool.
2 mL	½ tsp.	Granulated sugar	Mix remaining sugar and cinnamon together. Sprinkle over pie. Yield: 1 pie.
0.5 mL	⅛ tsp.	Cinnamon	

Pictured on cover.

Chocolate Chess Pie

This satisfying pie has a creamy chocolate flavor.

3	3	Large eggs	Beat eggs in mixing bowl
250 mL	1 cup	Granulated sugar	until frothy. Add next 7 ingre-
60 mL	¼ cup	Cocoa	dients. Beat to mix.
30 mL	2 tbsp.	All-purpose flour	
125 mL	½ cup	Milk	
60 mL	¼ cup	Butter or hard margarine, melted	
15 mL	1 tbsp.	White vinegar	
5 mL	1 tsp.	Vanilla	
125 mL	½ cup	Chopped pecans or walnuts (optional but good)	Stir in pecans.
1	1	Unbaked 9 inch (22 cm) pie shell	Pour into pie shell. Bake in 350°F (175°C) oven for 35 to 45 minutes until set. Yield: 1 pie.

Pictured below.

Plate Courtesy Of:
Ikea

Mock Mince Pie

Unbelievable! You can't tell it isn't mincemeat. Economical and very good. For a milder flavor, mix in ½ cup (125 mL) of applesauce.

250 mL	1 cup	Dry bread crumbs	Measure first 7 ingredients into bowl. Stir well.
250 mL	1 cup	Granulated sugar	
300 mL	1¼ cups	Raisins	
5 mL	1 tsp.	Cinnamon	
5 mL	1 tsp.	Nutmeg	
5 mL	1 tsp.	Cloves	
2 mL	½ tsp.	Salt	
250 mL	1 cup	Boiling water	In another bowl mix next 3 ingredients. Add to first bowl of dry ingredients. Stir. Let stand at least 30 minutes to allow bread crumbs and raisins to absorb some liquid.
125 mL	½ cup	Mild molasses	
60 mL	¼ cup	White vinegar	
		Pastry for 2 crust pie	Roll out pastry and line 9 inch (22 cm) pie plate. Roll out top crust. Turn filling into pie shell. Dampen edge of pastry. Cover with top crust. Trim. Crimp to seal. Cut vents in top.
2 mL	½ tsp.	Granulated sugar	Sprinkle with remaining sugar. Bake on bottom shelf in 400°F (205°C) oven for about 35 minutes until browned. Yield 1 pie.

Pictured on page 41.

Lemon Mousse Pie *A fluffy pie. Tart lemon flavor.*

5	5	Eggs yolks (large)	Beat egg yolks and sugar in top of double boiler until thick and piles softly.
175 mL	¾ cup	Granulated sugar	
100 mL	6 tbsp.	Lemon juice	Add lemon juice and rind. Stir over boiling water until it thickens. This will take about 10 minutes. Cool 10 minutes on counter.
5 mL	1 tsp.	Grated lemon rind	
5	5	Egg whites (large), room temperature	Beat egg whites in mixing bowl until stiff. Fold into hot mixture.
1	1	Baked 9 inch (22 cm) pie shell	Pile into pie shell. Bake in 350°F (175°C) oven for 15 minutes until golden brown. Cool.
		Whipped cream, page 61, for garnish	Garnish with whipped cream and grated chocolate. Yield: 1 pie.
5 mL	1 tbsp.	Grated chocolate, for garnish	

Pictured below.

Plate Courtesy Of:
Stokes

Date Pie
This is a grand pie. Best with whipped cream.

1	1	Large egg	Beat egg in bowl until frothy.
250 mL	1 cup	Sour cream	Beat in next 6 ingredients.
250 mL	1 cup	Brown sugar, packed	
0.5 mL	⅛ tsp.	Salt	
5 mL	1 tsp.	Brandy flavoring	
1 mL	¼ tsp.	Cinnamon	
0.5 mL	⅛ tsp.	Nutmeg	
375 mL	1½ cups	Chopped dates	Add dates and walnuts. Stir.
125 mL	½ cup	Chopped walnuts	
1	1	Unbaked 9 inch (22 cm) pie shell	Turn into pie shell. Bake on bottom shelf in 400°F (205°C) oven for 10 minutes. Reduce heat to 325°F (160°C). Continue to bake for 30 to 40 minutes until set. Cool. Cover with Whipped Cream, below.

Pictured on cover.

Whipped Cream

250 mL	1 cup	Whipping cream (or 1 envelope topping)	Beat all ingredients together until stiff. Yield: 2 cups (500 mL).
10 mL	2 tsp.	Granulated sugar	
5 mL	1 tsp.	Vanilla	

Makana Pie
Let everyone wonder what is in this delectable pie. Amazing.

125 mL	½ cup	Pineapple juice	Combine pineapple juice and lemon juice in large bowl. Add banana. Stir so all slices are coated. Let stand for 20 to 30 minutes.
1	1	Juice of lemon	
900 mL	4 cups	Sliced green tipped bananas (about 6 medium)	
		Pastry for 2 crust pie	Roll pastry and line 9 inch (22 cm) pie plate. Roll top crust. Remove banana slices with slotted spoon and put into pie shell. Reserve juice.
175 mL	¾ cup	Granulated sugar	Stir first amount of sugar, flour and cinnamon together in cup. Sprinkle over banana.
60 mL	¼ cup	All-purpose flour	
5 mL	1 tsp.	Cinnamon	
30 mL	2 tbsp.	Reserved juice	Drizzle reserved juice over top. Dot with butter. Dampen edge of crust. Cover with pastry. Trim and crimp to seal. Cut slits in top.
10 mL	2 tsp.	Butter or margarine	
2 mL	½ tsp.	Granulated sugar	Sprinkle with remaining sugar. Bake on bottom shelf in 400°F (205°C) oven for 30 to 40 minutes until browned. Do not freeze.
		Whipped Cream (see page 61), optional	Serve warm topped with Whipped Cream. Yield: 1 pie.

Pictured on page 63.

Pecan Sour Cream Pie

Contains pecans rather than the usual raisins. Put dollops of whipped cream on top for looks and taste.

2	2	Large eggs	Beat eggs in bowl until frothy. Beat in next 6 ingredients in order given.
15 mL	1 tbsp.	All-purpose flour	
1 mL	¼ tsp.	Cinnamon	
1 mL	¼ tsp.	Nutmeg	
250 mL	1 cup	Granulated sugar	
10 mL	2 tsp.	Lemon juice	
250 mL	1 cup	Sour cream	
250 mL	1 cup	Coarsely chopped pecans	Stir in pecans.
1	1	Unbaked 9 inch (22 cm) pie shell Whole pecans, for garnish	Turn into pie shell. Bake on bottom shelf in 350°F (175°C) oven for 35 to 40 minutes until set. Garnish with whole pecans. Yield: 1 pie.

1. Makana Pie page 62
2. Pecan Sour Cream Pie page 63

Serving Tray Courtesy Of:
Reed's China And Gift Shop

Pictured below.

Sweet Dream Squares *A moist date and nutty flavor.*

4	4	Large eggs	Beat eggs in mixing bowl until frothy.

225 mL	1 cup	Graham cracker crumbs	Stir in remaining ingredients in order given. Turn into greased 9 x 9 inch (22 x 22 cm) pan. Bake in 350°F (175°C) oven for about 30 minutes until an inserted wooden pick comes out clean. Cool. Ice with Vanilla Butter Icing, below. Cuts into 36 squares.
225 mL	1 cup	Brown sugar, packed	
5 mL	1 tsp.	Baking powder	
225 mL	1 cup	Chopped dates	
225 mL	1 cup	Chopped walnuts	

Vanilla Butter Icing

350 mL	1½ cups	Icing (confectioner's) sugar	Beat all ingredients together adding more or less liquid as needed. Spread over top.
30 mL	2 tbsp.	Butter or hard margarine, softened	
2 mL	½ tsp.	Vanilla	
30 mL	2 tbsp.	Milk or water	

Pictured on page 65.

Silver Trays Courtesy Of:
Sears Canada Inc.

Layered Brownies

An oatmeal base, chewy brownie center and chocolate icing.

Bottom Layer

175 mL	¾ cup	All-purpose flour
175 mL	¾ cup	Rolled oats
125 mL	½ cup	Brown sugar, packed
2 mL	½ tsp.	Baking soda
1 mL	¼ tsp.	Salt
125 mL	½ cup	Butter or hard margarine, melted

Stir first 5 ingredients together well. Mix in melted butter. Press into greased 9 x 9 inch (22 x 22 cm) pan. Bake in 350°F (175°C) oven for 10 minutes.

Top Layer

2 x 28 g	2 x 1 oz.	Unsweetened chocolate baking squares, cut up
125 mL	½ cup	Butter or hard margarine

Melt chocolate and butter in saucepan over low heat, stirring often. Remove from heat.

175 mL	¾ cup	Granulated sugar
2	2	Large eggs
175 mL	¾ cup	All-purpose flour
0.5 mL	⅛ tsp.	Salt
125 mL	½ cup	Chopped walnuts (optional)

With spoon, beat in sugar. Beat in eggs 1 at a time. Stir in flour, salt and walnuts. Spoon over bottom layer. Bake for about 25 minutes. An inserted wooden pick inserted near center should come out clean but moist. Cool.

Chocolate Icing

350 mL	1½ cups	Icing (confectioner's) sugar
75 mL	⅓ cup	Cocoa
50 mL	3 tbsp.	Butter or hard margarine, softened
30 mL	2 tbsp.	Hot water

Mix all ingredients in bowl, adding more or less water for spreading consistency. Spread over top. Cuts into 36 squares.

Pictured on page 65.

Date And Nut Squares
A good lunch box addition or with a cup of tea.

125 mL	½ cup	Butter or hard margarine, softened	Cream butter and both sugars together well. Beat in egg and vanilla.
75 mL	⅓ cup	Brown sugar, packed	
75 mL	⅓ cup	Granulated sugar	
1	1	Large egg	
5 mL	1 tsp.	Vanilla	
250 mL	1 cup	All-purpose flour	Mix in flour, baking powder and salt.
5 mL	1 tsp.	Baking powder	
2 mL	½ tsp.	Salt	
250 mL	1 cup	Chopped dates	Stir in dates and walnuts. Spread in greased 9 x 9 inch (22 x 22 cm) pan. Bake in 350°F (175°C) oven for about 25 to 30 minutes until set and browned. Cuts into 36 squares.
125 mL	½ cup	Chopped walnuts	

Pictured on page 65.

Sesame Squares
Great color. Crunchy and delectable.

2	2	Large eggs	Beat eggs in bowl until frothy. Add sugar. Beat well. Beat in butter.
500 mL	2 cups	Brown sugar, packed	
250 mL	1 cup	Butter or hard margarine, softened	
250 ml	1 cup	All-purpose flour	Add remaining ingredients. Stir. Spread in greased 10 x 15 inch (25 x 38 cm) jelly roll pan. Bake in 325°F (160°C) oven for 30 to 35 minutes or until center is set. Cool. Cuts into 48 bars.
2 mL	½ tsp.	Salt	
375 mL	1½ cups	Sesame seeds	

Pictured on page 65.

Caramel Almond Squares *Crunchy good.*

350 mL	1½ cups	All-purpose flour	Measure first 7 ingredients
125 ml	½ cup	Brown sugar, packed	into bowl. Mix until crumbly.
1	1	Large egg	Press into ungreased 9 x 9 inch
125 mL	½ cup	Butter or hard margarine, softened	(22 x 22 cm) pan. Bake in 350°F (175°C) oven for 20 minutes.
5 mL	1 tsp.	Baking powder	
5 mL	1 tsp.	Vanilla	
1 mL	¼ tsp.	Salt	

Topping

| 125 mL | ½ cup | Butter or hard margarine | Stir butter and sugar in |
| 75 mL | ⅓ cup | Brown sugar, packed | saucepan. Bring to a boil, stirring occasionally. Boil for 3 minutes. Pour over bottom layer. |

| 60 mL | ¼ cup | Sliced almonds | Sprinkle with almonds. Bake 7 minutes more. Cuts into 36 squares. |

Pictured below.

Cheesy Chip Squares

A chocolate base with a cheesy center topped with chocolate chips and pecans. Rich and delicious.

First Layer

300 mL	1 ¼ cups	All-purpose flour	Measure first 6 ingredients into bowl. Stir well.
250 mL	1 cup	Granulated sugar	
60 mL	¼ cup	Cocoa	
5 mL	1 tsp.	Baking powder	
5 mL	1 tsp.	Baking soda	
2 mL	½ tsp.	Salt	
1	1	Large egg	Add egg and butter. Mix. Press into greased 9 x 13 inch (22 x 33 cm) pan.
125 mL	½ cup	Butter or hard margarine, softened	

Second Layer

250 g	8 oz.	Cream cheese, softened	Beat cream cheese and sugar together well. Beat in eggs 1 at a time at medium-low speed. Add vanilla. Stir. Spread over first layer.
700 mL	3 cups	Icing (confectioner's) sugar	
2	2	Large eggs	
2 mL	½ tsp.	Vanilla	

Third Layer

175 mL	¾ cup	Chopped pecans (or walnuts)	Sprinkle pecans over top. Sprinkle chocolate chips over pecans. Bake in 350°F (175°C) oven for 25 minutes. Will rise on sides. Better made a day ahead. Cuts into 54 squares.
250 mL	1 cup	Semisweet chocolate chips	

Pictured on page 65.

Mint Brownies
Moist and minty. Mint can be omitted to make a regular brownie.

125 mL	½ cup	Butter or hard margarine
125 mL	½ cup	Granulated sugar
125 mL	½ cup	Brown sugar, packed
28 g	1 oz.	Unsweetened chocolate baking square, cut up
2	2	Large eggs
200 mL	¾ cup	All-purpose flour
5 mL	1 tsp.	Vanilla
0.5 mL	⅛ tsp.	Peppermint flavoring
125 mL	½ cup	Chopped almonds (or walnuts)

Choco Mint Icing

250 mL	1 cup	Semisweet chocolate chips
75 mL	⅓ cup	Evaporated milk
1 mL	¼ tsp.	Peppermint flavoring

Put butter, both sugars and chocolate into large saucepan. Heat and stir over medium-low heat until butter and chocolate melt. Remove from heat.

Add next 5 ingredients. Mix. Pour into greased 8 x 8 inch (20 x 20 cm) pan. Bake in 350°F (175°C) oven for about 25 minutes until an inserted wooden pick comes out clean but moist.

Place all 3 ingredients in saucepan. Heat and stir to melt chips. Cool. Spread over squares. Let stand for icing to set. Cuts into 36 squares.

Pictured on this page.

Trivet Courtesy Of:
Call The Kettle Black

Raisin Bar

A rich tasting square with a soft top and bottom crust.

250 mL	1 cup	Butter or hard margarine, softened	Place first 4 ingredients in bowl. Cut in butter until crumbly.
500 mL	2 cups	All-purpose flour	
250 mL	1 cup	Granulated sugar	
5 mL	1 tsp.	Baking soda	
1	1	Large egg, beaten	Add egg. Stir well. Press slightly more than ½ of crumbs into ungreased 9 x 9 inch (22 x 22 cm) pan.

Filling

125 mL	½ cup	Brown sugar	Stir sugar and flour thoroughly in saucepan. Mix in water and lemon juice. Add raisins. Heat and stir until it boils and thickens. Spoon over crust in pan. Scatter remaining crumbs over top. Bake in 350°F (175°C) oven for 25 to 30 minutes until light brown. Cuts into 36 squares.
30 mL	2 tbsp.	All-purpose flour	
125 mL	½ cup	Water	
15 mL	1 tbsp.	Lemon juice	
350 mL	1½ cups	Raisins	

Pictured on page 65.

Mock Chocolate Bar *A chewy delight.*

175 mL	¾ cup	Butter or hard margarine
60 mL	¼ cup	Smooth peanut butter
60 mL	¼ cup	Corn syrup
5 mL	1 tsp.	Vanilla

Combine first 4 ingredients in large saucepan. Heat and stir to melt. Remove from heat.

| 900 mL | 4 cups | Rolled oats (not instant) |
| 250 mL | 1 cup | Brown sugar, packed |

Stir in rolled oats and sugar. Pack in greased or foil lined 9 x 13 inch (22 x 33 cm) pan. Bake in 350°F (175°C) oven for about 15 minutes. Cool.

Icing

250 mL	1 cup	Semisweet chocolate chips
125 mL	½ cup	Butterscotch chips
125 mL	½ cup	Smooth peanut butter

Place both kinds of chips and peanut butter in saucepan. Heat and stir over low heat until melted. Spread over top. Cuts into 54 squares.

Pictured below.

Trivets Courtesy Of:
Stokes

Shattered Dreams

A coconut lemon square with a meringue-like topping that shatters easily. Scrumptious.

First Layer

350 mL	1½ cups	All-purpose flour
125 mL	½ cup	Brown sugar, packed
5 mL	1 tsp.	Baking power
125 mL	½ cup	Butter or hard margarine, softened
1	1	Large egg
5 mL	1 tsp.	Vanilla
1 mL	¼ tsp.	Salt

Mix all ingredients in bowl until crumbly. Pack into 9 x 13 inch (22 x 33 cm) ungreased pan.

Second Layer

2	2	Large eggs
125 mL	½ cup	Granulated sugar
50 mL	3 tbsp.	Lemon juice
30 mL	2 tbsp.	Butter or hard margarine

Beat eggs in top of double boiler (preferably not aluminum) until frothy. Add sugar, lemon juice and butter. Heat and stir until it thickens. Spread over first layer.

Third Layer

1	1	Large egg
150 mL	⅔ cup	Granulated sugar
225 mL	1 cup	Medium grated coconut

Beat egg in bowl. Beat in sugar. Stir in coconut. Spoon over second layer. Bake in 350°F (175°C) oven for about 20 minutes until set. Cuts into 54 squares.

1. Shattered Dreams page 73
2. Mock Chocolate Bar page 72

Pictured on page 72.

Black Forest Squares

With enough pieces to feed the whole gang.

1	1	Devils' Food cake mix, 2 layer size	Combine first 4 ingredients in bowl. Mix with a spoon. Spread in greased 10 x 15 inch (20 x 38 cm) jelly roll pan. Bake in 350°F (175°C) oven for 25 to 30 minutes. Cool.
2	2	Large eggs	
540 mL	19 oz.	Cherry pie filling	
5 mL	1 tsp.	Almond flavoring	

Icing

250 mL	1 cup	Semisweet chocolate chips	Place chocolate chips, butter and milk in saucepan. Heat and stir until chips are melted. Remove from heat.
30 mL	2 tbsp.	Butter or hard margarine	
60 mL	¼ cup	Milk	
250 mL	1 cup	Icing (confectioner's) sugar	Stir in icing sugar. Spread over top. Cuts into 60 squares.

Pictured below.

Measurement Tables

Throughout this book measurements are given in Conventional and Metric measure. To compensat_ for differences between the two measurements due to rounding, a full metric measure is not always used. The cup used is the standard 8 fluid ounce. Temperature is given in degrees Fahrenheit and Celsius. Baking pan measurements are in inches and centimetres. An exact metric conversion is given below as well as the working equivalent (Standard Measure).

SPOONS

Conventional Measure	Metric Exact Conversion Millilitre (mL)	Metric Standard Measure Millilitre (mL)
1/4 teaspoon (tsp.)	1.2 mL	1 mL
1/2 teaspoon (tsp.)	2.4 mL	2 mL
1 teaspoon (tsp.)	4.7 mL	5 mL
2 teaspoons (tsp.)	9.4 mL	10 mL
1 tablespoon (tbsp.)	14.2 mL	15 mL

CUPS

1/4 cup (4 tbsp.)	56.8 mL	50 mL
1/3 cup (5 1/3 tbsp.)	75.6 mL	75 mL
1/2 cup (8 tbsp.)	113.7 mL	125 mL
2/3 cup (10 2/3 tbsp.)	151.2 mL	150 mL
3/4 cup (12 tbsp.)	170.5 mL	175 mL
1 cup (16 tbsp.)	227.3 mL	250 mL
4 1/2 cups	1022.9 mL	1000 mL (1 L)

CASSEROLES (Canada & Britain)

Standard Size Casserole	Exact Metric Measure
1 qt. (5 cups)	1.13 L
1 1/2 qts. (7 1/2 cups)	1.69 L
2 qts. (10 cups)	2.25 L
2 1/2 qts. (12 1/2 cups)	2.81 L
3 qts. (15 cups)	3.38 L
4 qts. (20 cups)	4.5 L
5 qts. (25 cups)	5.63 L

CASSEROLES (United States)

Standard Size Casserole	Exact Metric Measure
1 qt. (4 cups)	900 mL
1 1/2 qts. (6 cups)	1.35 L
2 qts. (8 cups)	1.8 L
2 1/2 qts. (10 cups)	2.25 L
3 qts. (12 cups)	2.7 L
4 qts. (16 cups)	3.6 L
5 qts. (20 cups)	4.5 L

DRY MEASUREMENTS

Conventional Measure Ounces (oz.)	Exact Conversion Grams (g)	Standard Measure Grams (g)
1 oz.	28.3 g	30 g
2 oz.	56.7 g	55 g
3 oz.	85.0 g	85 g
4 oz.	113.4 g	125 g
5 oz.	141.7 g	140 g
6 oz.	170.1 g	170 g
7 oz.	198.4 g	200 g
8 oz.	226.8 g	250 g
16 oz.	453.6 g	500 g
32 oz.	907.2 g	1000 g (1 kg)

PANS

Conventional Inches	Metric Centimetres
8x8 inch	20x20 cm
9x9 inch	22x22 cm
9x13 inch	22x33 cm
10x15 inch	25x38 cm
11x17 inch	28x43 cm
8x2 inch round	20x5 cm
9x2 inch round	22x5 cm
10x4 1/2 inch tube	25x11 cm
8x4x3 inch loaf	20x10x7 cm
9x5x3 inch loaf	22x12x7 cm

OVEN TEMPERATURES

Fahrenheit (°F)	Celsius (°C)
175°	80°
200°	95°
225°	110°
250°	120°
275°	140°
300°	150°
325°	160°
350°	175°
375°	190°
400°	205°
425°	220°
450°	230°
475°	240°
500°	260°

Index

78